PIRATE'S GOLD

Henry Huttleston Rogers

Andrew Coe

presents

The Rogers Family

in

PIRATE'S GOLD

FOUR WINDS

PRESS

Four Winds Press
San Francisco, CA
FourWindsPress.com

ISBN: 978-1-940423-16-6

Cover and interior design by Susan Newman Design Inc.
Cover photo colorizations by Mark Lerer

Distributed by Publishers Groups West

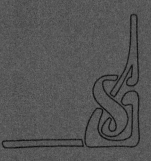

"I never heard about that!" said my father.

That was back in the days when the best way to look at old newspapers was on microfilm. I was cranking through reels of tape looking for historical nuggets on some other topic, when I ran across a big front-page headline containing the words "Rogers" and "Murder!" In 1935, a millionaire playboy named Henry H. Rogers III had been arrested on suspicion of murdering a Broadway actress. "Henry Rogers," I thought. "I wonder...." Reading down, I saw that the article mentioned his sister, the fashion icon Millicent Rogers, and his Robber Baron grandfather, Henry Huttleston Rogers, who helped build Standard Oil. Wow, I thought, that was MY family. I had always thought that my paternal ancestors had epitomized WASP respectability. Now I knew that at least one episode in the family's past had unreeled with all the elements (secluded farmhouse, booze, guns, sex, and desperation) of some cheap Hollywood crime drama.

I mailed a printout of the front-page to my father. He had been six in 1935 but never heard a peep about this family scandal. He realized that his parents not only hid all newspapers with headlines like "JAIL ROGERS IN SINGER'S DEATH" and "Drinking For A Week, Says

Shocked Cook," they also never mentioned the name of Henry Rogers III—his father's first cousin. Millions of Americans had lapped up the details about Rogers' involvement in the shooting of a Broadway actress, but my father had been kept blissfully unaware.

While working on other projects over the years, I continued to dig for more information about Henry Rogers III's drunken escapades. I soon learned that this wasn't the only Rogers family scandal. Back in 1924, young Millicent had eloped with Count Salm, a near-destitute Austrian Lothario twice her age. The tabloid saga of the Salm-Rogers marriage had kept readers riveted for years until they finally divorced. My research then led to Colonel Henry H. Rogers Jr., Millicent and Henry III's strict father, who thought he could rule his children with military discipline. Finally, I arrived at where the entire history started: the life of Henry Huttleston Rogers, the brilliant, ruthless financial genius who built one of the great American fortunes. After H. H. Rogers died in 1909, his will gave a mountain of money to his offspring. That's where the problems began.

I don't remember when I realized that there was money in my family. It was not in my immediate family. My father was a professor; we lived in a big, old drafty house in a college town; and we drove around in a VW bus. But my paternal grandparents owned a hilltop estate in Mill Neck, on Long Island's Gold Coast, which I remember for its swimming pool surrounded by boxwood hedges. Ever since, I've associated the scent of boxwood with wealth. Winters, we visited my grandparents in Hobe Sound, an enclave north of Palm Beach that didn't allow journalists, movie stars, Italians, Jews, or blacks to become property owners. We children were excited when they met us at the West Palm Beach airport in their Rolls-Royce Silver Cloud with tray tables that folded down from the back of the front seats. I liked fishing for grunts from their dock. Otherwise, to a child like me being rich seemed boring, an endless round of martinis and golf and going to the club.

The family's wealth was also enjoyed by the other members of my grandparents' generation. I worked one summer on my great uncle's ranch in the Wyoming Rockies. He visited for only a month or two every year from France, accompanied by a retinue that included his valet, a French chef and his wife, and a housekeeper—all for the upkeep of one elderly retired diplomat in a sprawling log cabin mansion. When I went to Rome, I stayed at my great aunt the Contessa's palazzo. My first morning there, the butler brought me breakfast in bed. This was the first time I had ever been waited on by a servant, and I realized that I hated it. My older relatives lived surrounded by wealth and luxury, but they were also trapped by it. They didn't need to work or really do anything at all but ring the bell and have a maid bring them another highball.

After I became a writer, I delved into my family's financial history. Tracing the lives of my ancestors, I began to see that being born to wealth had side effects other than status, power, and a life of luxury. For the sons, the first question was why should they apply themselves at all? They already had as much money as they ever would need. But male heirs were also burdened by their obligation to protect and grow the family wealth. For them, the most acceptable professions were in finance or the law. Anything else (my father was an expert on ancient Mesoamerica) was a waste of time. Daughters' duty was to produce children and insure the family's social status into the next generation. The best way they could do this was to marry a mate of equal or higher station, perhaps even with an aristocratic title before his name. This calculation was so oriented to the bottom line that a Protestant bishop compared the High Society mating dance to the slave market of old Baghdad.

In most WASP families, these tensions played out behind closed doors, carefully hidden from the outside world. But the Rogers family, for a few generations at least, had a predilection for living high and large. Following their story is a little like going to an old movie house for the Saturday afternoon matinee.

As the projector sputters to life, first you see the newsreels. There's a jerky clip of Henry Huttleston Rogers from more than a century ago. The story follows him from a little whaling town to the top of Standard

Oil. He mugs for the camera with his best friend Mark Twain, before dying as one of the richest Americans who ever lived. Then the first feature starts—a silent drama about the doomed romance between Count Salm, a Continental swashbuckler in the Rudolph Valentino mold, and the beautiful, fabulously wealthy "Milli" Rogers, who turns out to be more independent than she first seems. Behind the scenes lurks her father, the strict, tight-fisted Colonel Rogers. The second feature is a 1930s crime drama, strictly B-movie fare, starring Harry Rogers III as a drunken, gun-loving playboy desperate for his father the Colonel's approval—and money. As his life spirals downward, Harry meets Evelyn Hoey, a Broadway has-been who wants just one more shot at stardom. Fueled by whiskey, guns, and despair, the climax comes late one night in a Pennsylvania farmhouse. There's a moral in all of this. But first you have to find a comfortable chair, put a bowl of popcorn by your side, and turn the page....

ACT ONE

"Pluck, Push, and Perseverance"

Benjamin Franklin advised young men:

"Remember that money begets money.
The more there is of it, the more
it produces every turning, so that
profits rise quicker and quicker."

This is the story of a small-town boy who followed that advice—and succeeded beyond his wildest dreams.

Many years later, the people of Fairhaven, Massachusetts claimed they saw early signs of Henry H. Rogers' head for business. Henry bought two pairs of skates from the blacksmith. He used one pair and loaned out the other for two cents an hour. Those lacking sufficient funds could rent one skate for a penny.

As he grew into manhood, Fairhaven became too small for his ambitions. He first looked to the sea for adventure.

Fairhaven's economy revolved around whaling—danger-filled voyages, often lasting years, that returned with whale oil for the nation's lamps.

Henry's father knew how little a whaling man earned and advised his son not to go to sea—unless he wanted to be poor for the rest of his life. Henry took a job on the local railroad.

Mornings he grabbed the first
copy of the newspaper, scanning
its pages for opportunity.

GREAT OIL DISCOVERIES IN WESTERN PENNSYLVANIA!

Western Pennsylvania and a portion of Ohio are rife with excitement. The grand discovery of the age is oil springs. The earth is bored and burrowed into every direction to pump out the subterranean fluid. The price of land has gone up, and the price of oil has not yet come down. Fortunes are made, in imagination, by multitudes, and farm work is forgotton in search for hidden treasures....

Like many, Henry Rogers caught "oil fever." At age 20, he trekked to the wilds of Pennsylvania. On the banks of Oil Creek, he and a friend built a makeshift oil refinery.

The valley reeked with the sulfurous
stench of crude petroleum.
Black clouds of smoke spewed
from every refinery chimney.

For Henry Rogers, that was
the smell of money.

Rogers thrived in the boom-and-bust world of the oil frontier. Towns with names like Pithole and Babylon sprang up overnight, filled with barrooms and brothels. Rogers had a knack for games of chance.

After a year in oil country, Rogers returned to Fairhaven with $30,000 in his pocket—a fortune. He married his childhood sweetheart, Abbie Gifford, daughter of a whaling captain.

They settled in a cottage built on a hillside above the oil wells, where Abbie raised two daughters. Henry's drive and acumen caught the eye of a New York oil man—Charles Pratt.

Pratt manufactured the best brand of illuminating oil then on the American market.

PRATT'S ASTRAL OIL.
LIGHT FOR THE MILLIONS!
WILL NOT EXPLODE.

The Rogers family moved to Brooklyn, where Henry took charge of the Pratt refinery. Within a few years, Charles Pratt had made Rogers his partner.

In 1872, Rogers & Pratt's business was rattled by the soaring price of shipping a barrel of oil. John D. Rockefeller, owner of a Cleveland refinery called Standard Oil, was behind the scheme.

A classmate remembered John D. as "sane in every way but one—he was money mad." Rockefeller cut a deal with the railways to raise his competitors' freight costs and force them out of business.

Henry Rogers led the fight against
Standard Oil and broke the scheme,
"leaving Mr. Rockefeller looking
rather blue." Rogers, then 35,
was clearly a man to watch.

But two years later, in the midst of the "Panic of 1874," Rogers & Pratt decided it was better to join than fight. They secretly sold out to Standard Oil in return for stock and seats on the board.

ORGANIZED UNDER THE MANUFACTURING LAWS OF OHIO

No. 293

STANDARD OIL COMPANY

CAPITAL STOCK
$3,500,000.
ALL PAID

35,000 SHARES.
$100 EACH.

This is to Certify, that *Trustees of Standard Oil Trust* is entitled to Thirty four thousand nine hundred ninety than Shares of One Hundred Dollars each in the Capital Stock of the **Standard Oil Company**, transferable on the Books of the Company in person or by Attorney only on the surrender of this Certificate and due payment of all liabilities on the part of the holder to the Company, subject to the provisions of Law and the By Laws of the Company. This Certificate is valued only when signed by the President and Secretary.

Cleveland O Dec 23 1882

H. M. Flagler   Sect

J. D. Rockefeller   Prest

Within 15 years, the company controlled
90 percent of the country's petroleum
and most of its politicians.

Rogers rose to the top of the massive corporation. After Rockefeller retired, "the big brain, the big body, the head of Standard Oil, was Henry H. Rogers."

During the great anti-trust battles, he

became Standard's public face in its

fight against President Roosevelt.

Journalists called him "Hell-Hound Rogers" and portrayed him as a Jekyll and Hyde— both charming and ruthless. Cartoonists loved his magnificent moustache.

H. H. Rogers' fortune grew far beyond his childhood dreams. He lived with his family in a mansion just off Manhattan's Fifth Avenue.

The Rogers children were raised

with all the advantages of wealth.

Every summer, the family embarked on Rogers' 200-foot steam yacht *Kanawha*, the fastest private ship on water...

And sailed for his beloved
Fairhaven, where he had
built a summer "cottage."

A proud son of Fairhaven, H. H. Rogers

showered its citizens with his largesse.

He gave them a new Town Hall,...

A new library dedicated to the memory

of his daughter Millicent,

who died young,...

And a new high school, declared the finest school building in the United States.

Rogers' philanthropy also extended
to the larger world, almost always
anonymously. He helped fund
the construction of Booker T.
Washington's Tuskegee Institute.

He paid for the education of

Helen Keller.

And Rogers rescued the writer
Mark Twain from financial ruin. Both
small-town boys who made good, the
two became the closest of friends for
the last two decades of their lives.

Despite his philanthropy,

H. H. Rogers' wealth piled up faster

than he could give it away.

He still loved games of chance—from evening poker games to big bets on stocks that rocked Wall Street.

Railways...utilities...insurance companies—all were gaming chips to him. His greatest coup came when he wrested control of the world's largest copper mine at Butte, Montana.

LIFE

HENRY H. ROGERS
IN COPPER

OIL

THE ALCHEMIST

FROM A GRATE FUL PUBLIC

In 1904, he placed his biggest bet of all, deciding to build a railway from Appalachia to the sea. Wall Street "experts" predicted he would fail.

ROGERS LOSER
ON TIDEWATER

Virginia Project Has Cost Millions.

Oil Man Has Put Fourth of His Fortune Into It.

In 1909, workers drove the final
spike of what became the nation's
most profitable and efficient railway.
Rogers—with Twain at his side—
thumbed his nose at his doubters.

ROGERS OPENS HIS TIDEWATER ROAD WITH TWAIN'S AID

Sees Grand Climax of His Life's Work Carried to Final Completion

---

HUMORIST FRIEND GOBBLES APPLAUSE

Crowd Mistakes Distinguished Man of Letters for Man of Finance.

Six weeks later, H. H. Rogers was dead—
of a stroke early one morning.

HENRY H. ROGERS, FINANCIER, DIES SUDDENLY OF APOPLEXY

Head of the Amalgamated Copper Company and Vice President of Standard Oil Passes Away at His Home in New York Within an Hour After Complaining of Feeling Ill—His Career.

Obituary writers alternately praised
him for his brilliance in business
and philanthropy—and damned him
for his ruthlessness and greed.

"IN HIS CONTEMPT FOR LAW IN GREAT CAPITALISTIC ENTERPRISES, MR. ROGERS WAS UNQUESTIONABLY A PERIL, AND A MENACE TO OUR REPUBLIC."

At the news, flags in Fairhaven and Butte, Montana were flown at half staff. Leading financiers, the directors of Standard Oil, and Mark Twain mourned along with the Rogers family.

In Fairhaven, a huge crowd gathered in the pouring rain to see their benefactor interred in the Rogers mausoleum.

Henry Huttleston Rogers left one son,
three daughters, ten grandchildren,
and $49,000,000.

That money would be divided between the four branches of H. H. Rogers' descendants.

Benjamin

Rogers

Coe

Broughton

As the Rogers millions flowed down through the generations, each of his heirs would have to negotiate their own relationship with wealth. H. H. Rogers wore his fortune lightly. His children and grandchildren, however, would discover that riches defined them.

Their struggle would be to become
more than just "Standard Oil heirs."
This story will look at the patriarch's
legacy as it passed through one branch
of his descendants—the Rogers.

The Rogers Branch:

Henry H. Rogers Jr. ——— Mary Benjamin Rogers

Millicent Rogers   Henry H. Rogers III

End of
ACT ONE

ACT TWO

"Diamonds, and the Ritz"

On January 8, 1924, the line at the Marriage License Bureau in New York City's Municipal Building included a mechanic, a waiter, and two clerks accompanied by their spouses-to-be.

The next couple who entered the room
caused heads to turn. The man looked
like Rudolph Valentino, only better:
six feet tall, broad shouldered, with
brilliantined hair and a long face with
a prominent aristocratic nose.

His bride was slim, pale, and pretty,
her bobbed hair covered by a cloche hat
secured by a big, pearl-headed pin.
Bright dabs of rouge glowed on her lips.

She was wrapped in a lustrous
Russian sable coat probably worth
more than the combined assets of
everybody else in that room.

The groom swept up to the head
of the line, asking for the deputy
clerk. The couple was ushered to
his private office, where they filled
out the marriage certificate.

CERTIFICATE AND RECORD OF MARRIAGE

OF

(Groom) _Ludwig A. M. Salm_ and (Bride) _Marie H. Rogers_

Groom's Residence	707 Madison Ave.	Bride's Residence	Cor. Madison Ave.
Age	37	Age	21 — & 46 Street
Color	White	Color	White
Single, Widowed or Divorced	Divorced	Single, Widowed or Divorced	Single
Occupation	Antique dealer	Maiden Name, if a Widow	x
Birthplace	Germany	Birthplace	N.Y.C.
Father's Name	Alfred	Father's Name	Harry
Mother's Maiden Name	Adolfine Erlanger	Mother's Maiden Name	Mary Benjamin
Number of Groom's Marriage	Second	Number of Bride's Marriage	First

I hereby certify that the above-named groom and bride were joined in Marriage by me, in accordance with the Laws of the State of New York, at Municipal Building Manhattan _____ (Street) (Church), in the Borough of _____, City of New York, this 28 of January 1924

Signature of person performing the Ceremony _J. McCormick_

Witnesses to the Marriage: _Julius J. Brosey_ _Aladar G. Fisher_

Official Station: DEPUTY CITY CLERK
Residence: 3675 BROADWAY

RECEIVED FEB 19 1924 OFFICE OF THE REGISTRAR BOROUGH OF MANHATTAN

"Ludwig Salm," wrote the groom in a bold European scrawl. "Marie Henrietta Rogers," penned the bride—close enough to make it legal. The clerk and a witness also signed, and it was official.

WE hereby certify that we are the Groom and Bride named in this

Certificate, and that the information given therein is correct, to the best of

our knowledge and belief.

Imre Lakin Groom

Georgie Henrietta Kupo Bride

Signed in the presence of

Julius W. Brown

and

Aladar Geza Fisher

It shall be the duty of the clergymen, magistrates and other persons who perform the marriage ceremony to keep a registry of the marriages celebrated by them. * Every person authorized by law to perform the marriage ceremony shall register his or her name and address in the office of the Bureau of Records (Sec. 35, Sanitary Code).

It shall be the duty of every person required to make or keep any such registry, of * * * * * * * * marriage * * * * * * * * to present to the Bureau of Records a copy of such registry signed by such person * * * * * * * * * * * * within ten days after the * * * * * * * * marriage * * * * * * * * which shall thereupon be placed on file in the said Bureau (Sec. 33, Sanitary Code).

N. B.—Sec. 1239, Chap. 532, Laws of 1905, makes the failure to report within ten days a written copy of the registry of the marriages provided to be registered a misdemeanor, punishable by fine or imprisonment.

On January 8, 1924 Count Ludwig Albrecht
Constantin Maria von Salm Hoogstraeten
married Mary Millicent Rogers, the girl
with "The Diamond as Big as the Ritz."

Wedding
Congratulations

The hero in Fitzgerald's fable from *Tales of the Jazz Age* is a boarding school boy who goes to spend the summer with a rich classmate.

His family's home is a chateau high in the Rockies that rests upon the source of its wealth: a diamond as big as the Ritz-Carlton Hotel.

Our hero discovers a horrible secret:

No one who learns of the diamond is

allowed to leave the mountain alive.

His fate is averted when Air Force

biplanes materialize over the chateau.

The family tries to repel them with

a barrage of antiaircraft fire.

The planes retaliate with a rain of bombs that destroys this secret Eden. As our hero flees across the barren foothills, he realizes that the rest of his life will only bring disillusionment and poverty.

Count Ludwig Salm was not a callow youth.

He had already been married and divorced.

As an Austro-Hungarian Army officer,

he had fought in the Great War—

and survived a duel at dawn.

Count Salm's only lack was money. After the war, Austria's economy was in ruins. He decided to try his luck in America. His dream was to marry a rich American woman. In 1923, he sailed for New York City.

S. S. "PRESIDENT HARDING."

"U. S. LINER."

The Count checked into that
oasis of European sophistication:
the Ritz-Carlton Hotel.

Ah, the Ritz—the best food, the
best people, the best service! The
Count liked to stop off for a smoke
in the hotel's Palm Court.

One night, Count Salm noticed a young
woman sitting at the next table. He
recognized her face from a society dance.
Their eyes met. She asked:
"Would you care for a cigarette?"

Millicent Rogers, the granddaughter
of Henry Huttleston Rogers!

Millicent Rogers, the millionaire flapper!
This was the Jazz Age, when women
not only smoked in public but pursued
men. That evening, a few sparks were
lit that soon turned into a blaze.

The wheels of love spun quick
(particularly because Millicent and her
parents also occupied a suite in the Ritz).
Count Salm was too much a gentleman
to share details, except to say: "Once
there were two lonely little birds."

But after weeks of passion...discovery!
Friends noticed the Count's attentions
to "Milli" and informed her parents.
"That man," they told her, "is out of the
question." Millicent should start packing:
"In three days, we're leaving for Europe!"

Milli and "Ludi" realized that parting would be fatal to their love. They devised a plan: a City Hall wedding— and then present her parents with a *fait accompli*. Surely they would relent when they saw proof of their love.

Ludi did not doubt that he would be
accepted. Yes, Milli brought her millions
to the marriage. But Ludi gave her
the title of "Countess" and the Rogers
clan the honor of being linked to the
thousand-year-old lineage of Salm.

Milli broke the news to her parents at the Ritz. Minutes later she called the Count: "Very bad, Ludi darling!" Her father had refused to hear anything about a marriage, telling Milli: "Go to your room!" For him, it seemed, the real aristocracy was of money.

The next day, Milli's parents seemed to relent. They would go to their country estate and let the newlyweds use their suite. Ludi was packing, when seven reporters burst into his room: Ludi and Milli were NEWS!

NEW YORK HEIRESS TO $40,000,000 ESTATE WEDS AUSTRIAN NOBLEMAN

HEIRESS

MYSTERY

New York Society Is Still Dazed Over Marriage of Rogers' Heiress to Count

In the 1920s tabloid press, lurid tales about the rich and famous filled headlines. The Salm-Rogers affair was too juicy to ignore. Reporters raked over the Count's ancestry, his finances, his divorce, and his many loves.

COUNT SALM, ROAMING ROMEO

WAR OF T...

...E COUNT

ROMANCES HAVE COME OFTEN AND EASY TO COUNT SALM-HOOGSTRATEN OF LATE

Ludi and Milli were safe as long as they remained in the luxury and security of the Rogers suite. But every time they stepped out of the hotel, they were dogged by shutterbugs.

Worse, they were running out of money.
Her parents had cut off her allowance.
The only solution was to beg for help
from the man who controlled the purse
strings: Colonel Henry H. Rogers Jr.

Colonel Rogers was the only son and namesake of Henry Huttleston Rogers. He had been born with a platinum spoon in his mouth. He grew up to embody wealth and entitlement.

He worked in his father's office at
Standard Oil, but his true passion was
the military—the drills, the uniforms,
the barked orders to his troops.

After serving in World War I, he retired
at age 40, devoting the rest of his life
to enjoying his wealth—and guarding it
from men like Count Ludwig Salm.

Despite Milli's pleas, the Colonel refused
to meet Ludi. His secretary carried
the message: "Count Salm shall never
touch a penny of your grandfather's
estate, nor of mine, so long as I
live and control either estate."

Desperate, Ludi sold his story to a
newspaper for $2,500. Ghost-written
by an imaginative journalist, it ran
in Hearst's *New York American*
as a splashy 14-part series.

How I Wooed and Won the Heiress to the $40,000,000 Rogers Estate

By COUNT LUDWIG SALM VON HOOGSTRAETEN

Stonewalled by her father—hounded by reporters—Milli needed to escape. On a freezing January day, the newlyweds walked up the gangplank of an ocean liner, where they were ambushed by a horde of shutterbugs.

"Thus the honeymoon begins," wrote a journalist. "Millicent Rogers Salm and her noble Count o' Dreams, standing on the steamship *Veendam*, barely smiling farewell to America yesterday. Not a member of the Rogers clan, not a friend even, was at the pier to bid bon voyage."

When they reached France, bliss:
no reporters or photographers waited
on the docks to greet them! Carefree
days and nights—they traveled to the
Riviera, where Milli shopped while
Ludi, a tennis champion before the
war, trained for the Davis Cup.

In April, the newlyweds were
blessed with exciting news—
Milli was expecting their first child!

In May, a telegram caught up with them in Milan. They tore it open—to find an ominous portent for their future. Colonel Rogers—and his lawyer—would soon be in Paris. Hearing of her pregnancy, he wanted to see her at his hotel. Was this opportunity for reconciliation— or something else? Ludi was not invited.

The Colonel told Milli he only had her "best interests" at heart. He wanted her to have the baby in New York, where the family doctors could care for her. He hinted that he would also open the family coffers for her and Ludi.

The Colonel's lawyer met with Ludi.
The Colonel had no objection to Ludi...
only there was a problem with the
marriage papers. Had Ludi's first
marriage really been annulled? Milli
dreamed of a church wedding.

Reluctantly—and with many tears—
they agreed to part—but only for a few
brief weeks. Ludi took the first train
to Vienna to meet with his lawyer,
while Milli returned to New York with
the Colonel on the *S. S. France.*

1040   Le Paquebot Transatlantique " France "
Long. 220 m., larg., 23 m., tonnage 22.500 tonnes
Puissance 40.000 chevaux
Passagers, 534 de 1ʳᵉ classe, 412 de 2ᵉ, 226 de 3ᵉ,
724 de 4ᵉ
Etat-Major et Equipage, 600
Au total, 2.526 personnes à bord

Collection Delaveau-Joubier, St-Nazaire

Weeks dragged into months. Ludi and his lawyers struggled with Vatican bureaucracy. Milli once again enjoyed an allowance to spend on clothes and jewels—and the protection of the Rogers family's wealth and power.

Meanwhile, the tabloids filled their pages
with tales of the star-crossed lovers,
claiming that the Colonel had paid
Ludi to let Milli return to New York.

Rogers Pays Count $100,000
to Quit $40,000,000 Bride

5 CENTS PAY NO MORE **SUNDAY NEWS** **FINAL EDITION**

NEW YORK'S PICTURE NEWSPAPER

New York, Saturday, May 14, 1921

Vol. 1. No. 3. 12 Pages

SALM BOUGHT OFF

That was a lie: Ludi was in love and still believed he would be accepted by the Rogers family. Next, the Count received a terse telegram from Milli: "What is all this talk about Lya de Putti?"

Also untrue: The Count had never met the Hungarian vamp. An infatuated American reporter had invented a Lya-Ludi romance to help her career. Then came the stories about Ludi's behavior on the tennis court.

Alas, Ludi was guilty—he pled the
stress of being apart from Milli.
Then, in September, came a brief, happy
moment—the arrival of their little Peter.

Milli called him "Bunny." The tabloids dubbed him "The Richest Little Boy in the World."

BRITAIN TO AVENGE VERA

COUNT SALM'S BABY: THE PAWN IN A WAR OF TITLE VS. MILLIONS

Separated by an ocean, Ludi could
not secure a visa to see his newborn
son. (He suspected Rogers influence
at the U. S. consulate.) His every
move was dogged by a private
detective in the pay of the Colonel.

Ludi pressed on...but doubts began to gnaw away at Milli. Those tabloid stories...and the Colonel did not budge on the central point: Ludi would never be allowed to touch the Rogers fortune. In May of 1925—a year since they had parted—Ludi received a letter just as he was about to begin a Davis Cup match.

"Dear Ludi..."

Milli's love had turned into anger at Ludi—
for his "vagabond existence"—for the "other
women"—for writing news articles that
embarrassed her family—and for his inability
to hold a job. For all those reasons...

"That is that, Millicent."

"The very rich," said Fitzgerald, "are different from you and me." Milli was used to ease, to effortlessly gliding from one scene to another. Ludi's life was fraught—with bills, worries, having to do with less. Rather than live with difficulty, she had simply shut the door.

Ludi reeled, losing the first set of his tennis match 6-0. But a Salm would not give up! He was determined to fight for his son—and to repair his own, tarnished reputation. He came back to win the draw for Austria!

The fight against the Rogers lawyers
was a tougher war. Desperate to see
his son, Ludi sailed for New York.

White Star Line.

Ludi followed Milli to Palm Beach.
A court order opened the door for
a visitation. Photographers caught
the nurse—her hand shielding the
boy—Count Salm averting his face—
with bodyguards fore and aft.

The *affaire* Rogers vs. Salm moved
back to New York, where Ludi sued
for separation—and sole custody of
his son. To help readers catch up, the
Daily Mirror published a cartoon history
of the troubled romance: the couple's
fateful meeting...secret marriage...flight
to Europe...the Count is turned away
at Milli's door...and finally, the trial.

American Heiress and Titled Husband Wage Battle for Custody of Son

AT AN EARLY age Count Ludwig von Hoogstraeten was a Beau Brummel with the ladies. He was married, but a divorce followed. He went in for tennis and won championship rank. Then, he met Millicent Rogers, heiress to $40,000,000 made in Standard Oil.

SOCIETY of two continents was startled to hear of their secret marriage in the Municipal Building here, Jan. 8, 1924. Salm had been reported engaged to Mrs. Grace Coffin and he had dined with her the day before. The bride's family frowned upon the match.

THE NEWLYWEDS sailed for Europe, unforgiven. H. H. Rogers, Millicent's father, made a secret trip abroad, and he returned to the United States with his daughter. The Count was left in Paris. Soon afterward, Millicent gave birth to a son, Peter, now 2.

SALM, so he says, didn't believe Millicent was leaving him for good. He didn't find that out until he came back to the States with his mother and faced the closed Rogers door. He called his wife "heartless," and made numerous efforts to see his son.

NOW THE Count and Countess meet again in Supreme Court here. The Count has sued for separation, charging desertion. Millicent justifies her action on the plea of nonsupport. The real fight centers around the custody of the boy, Peter.

Ludi hoped the trial would restore his good name. But Milli's lawyers portrayed him as a "no account count" who could not support his wife in the manner she deserved. Ludi's testimony left him twisting and turning in the wind.

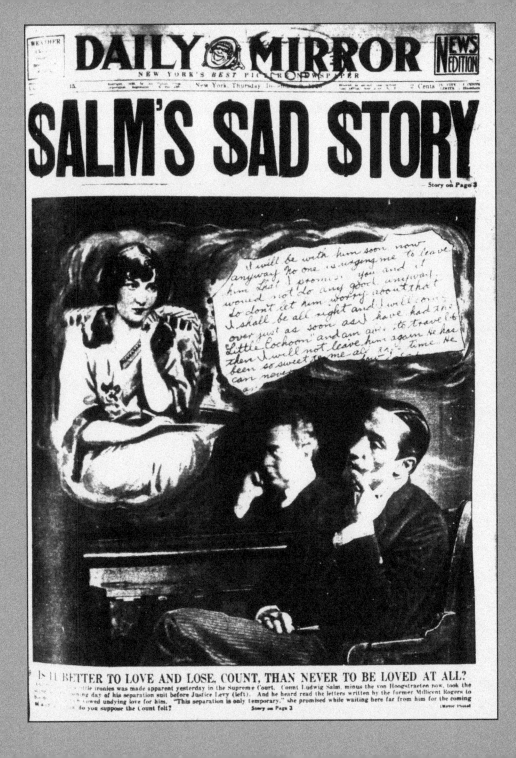

DAILY ◉ MIRROR

NEW YORK'S BEST PICTURE NEWSPAPER

NEWS EDITION

New York, Thursday ··· 2 Cents

ALM' $AD $TORY

Story on Page 3

IS IT BETTER TO LOVE AND LOSE, COUNT, THAN NEVER TO BE LOVED AT ALL?

... ttle ironies was made apparent yesterday in the Supreme Court. Count Ludwig Salm, minus the von Hoogstraeten now, took the ... ning day of his separation suit before Justice Levy (left). And he heard read the letters written by the former Millicent Rogers to ... vowed undying love for him. "This separation is only temporary," she promised while waiting here far from him for the coming ... do you suppose the Count felt? **Story on Page 3** (Mirror Photo)

Q: "Who paid the hotel bills for you and Countess Salm?"

A: "My wife."

Q: "Weren't you, then, just in it for the money?"

A (shouted): "I don't want money! I want my son! I'm no gold digger!"

But Ludi's lawyer had a surprise:

Milli's letters! A gasp went around

the courtroom as he began

to read: "Dear Ludi..."

"Don't worry about my parents. They will come around. In the meanwhile let's not cramp our style. Let's live in good hotels. I don't want you to work, especially in motion pictures."

Pfffft!—that was the sound of Milli as the aggrieved spouse being deflated. Their lawyers agreed on terms that evening. From New York, the case Salm vs. Salm moved to Paris. Early in 1927, they signed the divorce papers. They would share custody of young Peter. Ludi would recieve a payout—$325,000 rumors said. They were both now free to pursue new loves.

Zip! Zing! Decree! Divorce à la Française

Accounting for the Vogue of
A DIVORCE *in* PARIS

Easy Paris Divorce

Milli found Arturo Ramos, a handsome Argentine. *Variety* wrote: "Argentina has been furnishing Paris her very best gigolos. All the women who are really smart, really like Argentines. Millicent Rogers, who always does smart things no matter what people say, married one."

Ludi was seen around the watering holes with an American divorcée. His tennis career dwindling, he reinvented himself as a showbiz impresario. That ended when rumors of war killed tourism. Busted, he sued Milli and Peter for support—and lost. His son's guardians granted him a small allowance, but that ended in 1941.

The war trapped Ludi in Central Europe. In 1944, the Gestapo picked him up in Budapest and questioned him for three days. Afterward, he returned to his hotel—the Ritz.

Ludi drank a glass of wine at the
bar, then went up to his room. He
climbed onto the window sill and
jumped—five stories to his death.

End of
ACT TWO

ACT THREE

"Sins of the Father"

The Colonel and Mrs. Rogers also had a son. Henry H. Rogers III, known as "Harry," carried the family's glory in his name. But he was overshadowed by his pretty and precocious older sister.

Harry was a weedy and awkward boy.
He clung to his mother, earning
the scorn of his soldier father.

He liked to tinker with machines,
dreaming of an invention that
would make him rich and
famous like his grandfather.

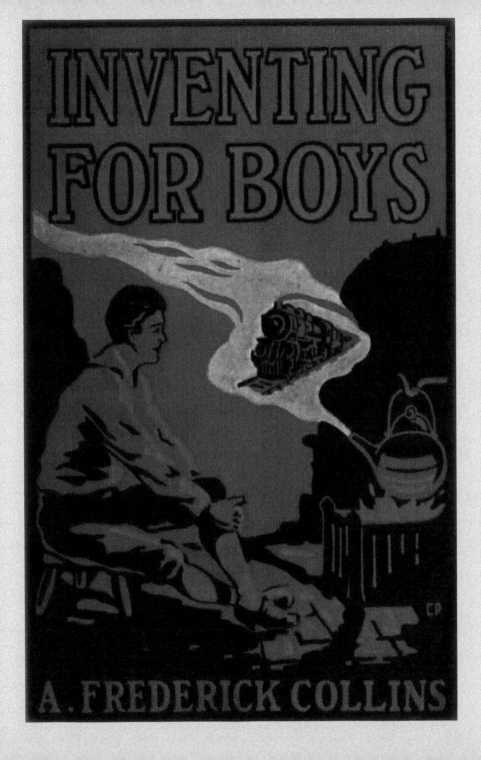

INVENTING FOR BOYS

A. FREDERICK COLLINS

At boarding school, his family's extreme wealth set him apart. One evening, the fellows compared allowances—50 cents to a dollar a week. Then came Harry's turn: "$12,000 a year." When Harry showed home movies of his family's estate and his sister posing on the grounds, they jeered: "That's not your sister—that's a movie actress. And that's a Hollywood set!"

He invited a friend home for vacation, showing him the fountains, servants, Rolls-Royces, tapestries, suits of armor— and his beautiful sister Millicent (like out of a Fitzgerald story). "Tell them," said Harry, "It's all true."

When Harry turned 18, the Colonel
decided that the best place for his son
was Oxford University. Harry made a life-
changing discovery in Oxford's pubs. "I'm
not much to look at," he told a friend,
"funny face, spectacles, thin body. If I
get a drink or two inside me it helps."

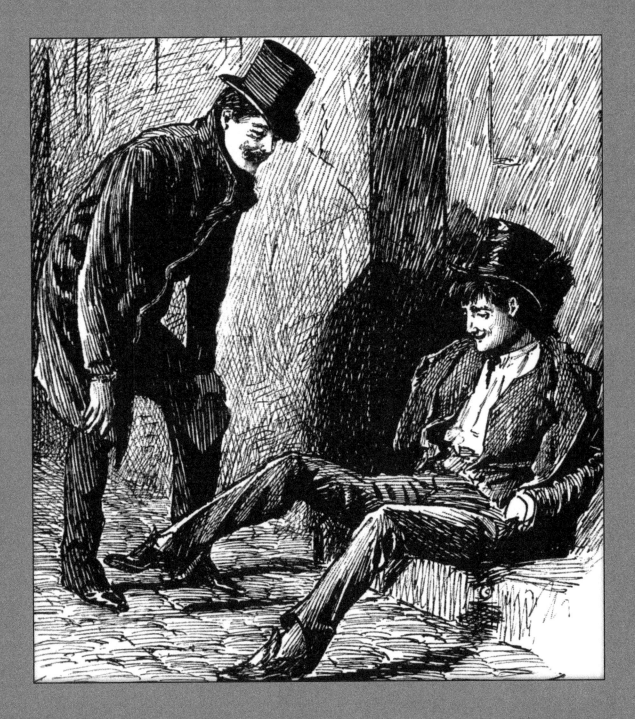

In 1927, Harry returned to the United States without taking a degree. Age 22, he decided his formal education was complete. He was determined to prove that he could become more than a "Rogers of Standard Oil."

Like his grandfather, Harry headed
West. He settled in Cleveland and
found a 25 cent an hour job tinkering
on transmissions (while still living off
his father's allowance). He married
Miss Virginia Lincoln, a local society girl.

The Colonel didn't attend the wedding,

too busy in Paris preparing to divorce

Harry and Millicent's mother.

He was romancing a comely Hungarian

widow, who became (for a few short years)

his second wife.

To celebrate their new life together, the
Colonel built a Hamptons pleasure palace
called the "Port of Missing Men."

It had bedrooms with names like
"Room of the Roman Virgins"
and an enormous indoor pool in
the style of ancient Pompeii.

The Great Depression killed Harry's Cleveland job. He and Virginia returned to New York, where he succumbed to the temptations of the Broadway lights.

Harry haunted the Big Apple's speakeasies and nightclubs. Dawn would find him showing off his skills in one of Times Square's seedy shooting galleries.

Enamored with show business—and show girls—Harry decided to go into the movie business. Bankrolled by the Colonel, his production company was grandly called...

STANDARD MOTION PICTURES, INC.

H. H. ROGERS, PRES.

Harry's first film, featuring two has-been vaudeville comedians, took advantage of the end of Prohibition.

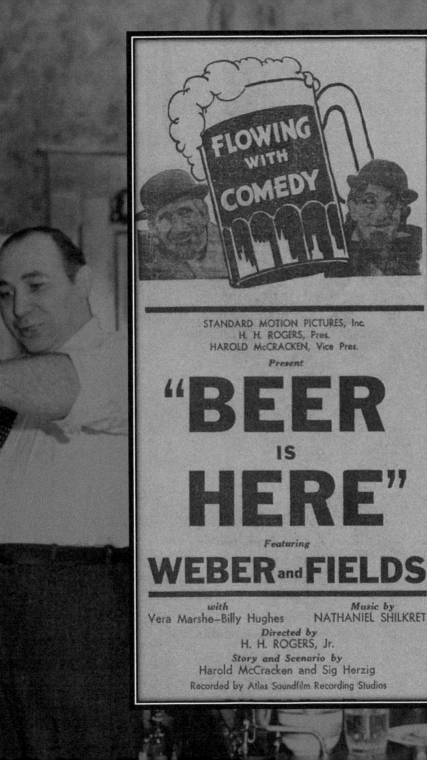

FLOWING
WITH
COMEDY

STANDARD MOTION PICTURES, Inc.
H. H. ROGERS, Pres.
HAROLD McCRACKEN, Vice Pres.

Present

"BEER IS HERE"

Featuring

WEBER and FIELDS

with
Vera Marshe – Billy Hughes

Music by
NATHANIEL SHILKRET

Directed by
H. H. ROGERS, Jr.

Story and Scenario by
Harold McCracken and Sig Herzig

Recorded by Atlas Soundfilm Recording Studios

Variety called it "inept" and a "grand bore."
Beer Is Here fell flat. Harry went back
to the Colonel to borrow more money
for his next film, a "nudist" comedy.

Written and directed by Harry,
Nearly Naked received all the ballyhoo
that Rogers money could generate.

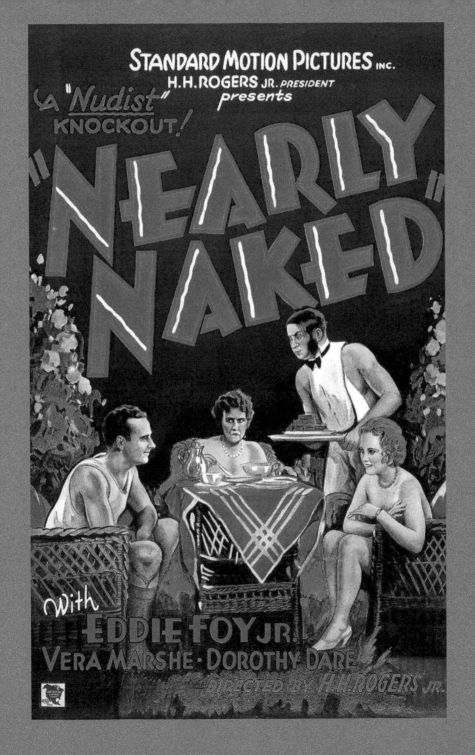

Variety was not impressed: "The H. H. Rogers firm...missed by a mile." Audiences agreed—the box office was dismal. Depressed, Harry began to hit the bottle even harder. Fed up, Virginia fled back to her parents in Cleveland.

Harry barely noticed. He went back to

his father, pleading for more money

to save Standard Motion Pictures.

But the Colonel refused, seeing Harry as a dissolute whose Hollywood dreams would never amount to anything. In drunken revenge—at a glittering dinner to celebrate the Colonel's engagement to his third wife, Pauline—Harry turned to his father and loudly exclaimed...

"For God's sake, can you stop hanging a marriage license on every woman you fuck?"

The next day the Colonel called
his lawyer. He wanted to revise...

The Last Will and Testament of Colonel Henry H. Rogers

A few months later, the Colonel's doctor, worried about his patient's persistent cough, sent him to Johns Hopkins. The country's top lung man diagnosed cancer. Four operations could not save the Colonel.

Colonel Henry H. Rogers Jr. died on July 25, 1935. After the funeral, his body was interred in the Rogers mausoleum—beneath his famous father.

The family then returned to the Port of Missing Men, where the library was set for the reading of the will. The Colonel's attorney, Adrian Larkin sat behind the desk. Facing him: the Colonel's widow Pauline, Millicent, and Harry.

The will hit its target early: Harry would not inherit any of the Rogers Trust. Instead, he would receive an income of $25,000 a year—chickenfeed for a Rogers. To the gasps of his audience, Larkin revealed that Harry's share in the Rogers trust would go to nine-year-old Peter Salm—the "Golden Boy."

Rogers' Heir Loses Riches To Salm's Son

OIL MAN'S HEIR

Henry H. Rogers, Jr.
He's cut off in will from father's estate.

The Colonel then turned his aim on Millicent and his widow Pauline. Like Harry, neither of them would touch the principal of the Rogers Trust. Each would receive $118,000 a year—a fortune, but not the expected pot of gold.

Rogers Will Is Laid to 'Sick Mind'

Lawsuits followed fast and furious,
but they could not break the Colonel's
will. In shock, Harry fled to the City,
where he consoled himself with
the bottle and his girlfriend, sultry
Broadway star Evelyn Hoey.

The showbiz trajectory of Evelyn Hoey: "Minneapolis to Broadway—top of the heap, a crown of glamour and bright lights....Then the lights dimming, the glamour fading." Age 24 and already washed-up, Evelyn Hoey met Harry Rogers, playboy producer. He promised to make her a movie star.

PHOTOPLAY

JUNE

25 CENTS
20 Cents in Canada

But after the reading of the will,
Harry was too upset to talk showbiz.
Lawyers were telling him that his case
was hopeless. Harry was going crazy—
he needed to get out of town.

Harry owned Indian Run Farm, a country retreat in Pennsylvania. He and Evelyn packed enough clothes and liquor to stay for an open-ended weekend party.

If Evelyn had been expecting a rural idyll, the arrival was a letdown. The house was a mess, with empty bottles everywhere, ashtrays filled with cigarette stubs, dishes piled in the sink.

Evelyn also learned that—aside from drinking—Harry's favorite pastime here was playing with his vast collection of armaments.

Harry opened a bottle of Scotch—and didn't stop drinking for the next week. The couple would usually wake up around noon and start drinking. Then, some nude swimming and sunbathing. Later, when things got hilarious, Harry would load up his Browning machine gun and blast away into the woods.

These sophisticated antics did not
go over well with the neighbors—
who steered clear of Indian Run
Farm for fear of their lives.

A week into their spree, Harry turned angry and morose. Fuming about the farm's condition, he wanted to meet with his lawyers about suing the foreman. But Evelyn didn't want the party to end. They began to fight.

Evelyn decided to go back to New York. She tried to borrow train fare from the chauffeur—Harry yelled at her. She ran upstairs to call her mother—Harry ran outside and yanked the telephone cable from the side of the house.

Harry came inside, the servants

later testified, and went upstairs....

After a minute or two—a shot!

The servants ran upstairs. Evelyn Hoey
lay on the bedroom floor—with a hole
in her temple and a pearl-handled
.45 caliber revolver by her side.

On the dresser stood a photograph
of Harry's revered grandfather,
Henry Huttleston Rogers, bearing
mute witness to this scene of
tragedy and degradation.

Because Harry had torn out the phone line, the chauffeur had to drive off to find a doctor—and call the police. By dawn, Henry H. Rogers III was under arrest. The charge was: suspicion of murder.

ROGERS JR. HELD IN EVELYN HOEY DEATH

Who Pulled the Trigger?

Where Death Joined Party

Rogers Jr.
ath of actress

Newspaper columnist Walter Winchell called it "one of those social smells"—and hinted that Harry's movie cameras were for making the kind of home movies that you don't show to mother.

Local police searched the house attempting to reconstruct Evelyn's death. Under a bed, they found a huge pile of photographs of "undraped women."

Harry got his one phone call and dialed his mother in New York. The family's high-powered lawyers sprung him on bail. He holed up at a nearby resort hotel to prepare for the inquest.

While Evelyn's grieving parents prepared
to bring her body home, Harry bought
an enormous wreath to be placed on
her casket. His lawyers made sure
a photographer was on hand.

The inquest was the biggest media
circus ever seen in Chester County,
Pennsylvania. People fought to
get into the courtroom.

A path was cleared for Harry's mother—
elegant in black and pearls—
accompanied by her New York lawyers.

A hidden camera smuggled into the courtroom captured Harry's reactions on the stand (and his mother).

Rogers Collapses
In Tears Telling Of
Evelyn Hoey Death

Harry insisted that Evelyn had shot herself—she had a history of suicidal behavior. The prosecutor grilled him:

Q: "Did you shoot Miss Hoey?"
A: "No! I'd do anything in the world for her. I'd give my life for her!"

OPEN VERDICT HANDED DOWN IN HOEY DEATH

Coroner's Jury, After 5 Hours, Files Finding of "Person or Persons Unknown"

Probe of Shooting, Also Drinking by Members of Panel Is to Be Continued

But the jury didn't buy Rogers' story, handing down a verdict of "death by person or persons unknown." Without new evidence, the judge let Rogers go free— trailed by a dark cloud of suspicion.

Two months later, the prosecutor tried again, impaneling a grand jury to hear the case. Rogers family lawyers made sure the jury heard all the evidence— their evidence. The Hoey family protested but the outcome was foregone.

EVELYN HOEY KILLED SELF, JURY DECIDES

Absolved by Jury

HENRY H. ROGERS 3rd.

Harry spent that winter in Miami, where he dove right back into the world of nightclubs and showgirls.

For Evelyn Hoey, however, there was only the silence of a tomb at St. Louis's Oak Grove Cemetery.

Evelyn Hoey

1910 — 1935

End of
ACT THREE

Epilogue

Money was the wind beneath the Rogers family wings. Even Harry had enough. In Miami, Harry met and married a hard-drinking former showgirl.

They ended up in Los Angeles, where
Harry tinkered with inventions and
attempted to get back into motion pictures.
But mostly he drank, succumbing
in 1948 to cirrhosis of the liver.

DISTRICT NO. 1901   REGISTRAR'S NO. 10620

1. FULL NAME   HENRY H ROGERS

2. PLACE OF DEATH: (A) COUNTY   Los Angeles
   (B) CITY OR TOWN   Los Angeles
   IF OUTSIDE CITY OR TOWN LIMITS, WRITE RURAL
   (C) NAME OF HOSPITAL OR INSTITUTION
   Cedars of Lebanon Hospital
   IF NOT IN HOSPITAL OR INSTITUTION, GIVE STREET NUMBER OR LOCATION
   (D) LENGTH OF STAY: (SPECIFY WHETHER YEARS, MONTHS OR DAYS)
   IN HOSPITAL OR INSTITUTION   1 day
   IN THIS COMMUNITY   10 yrs   IN CALIFORNIA   10 yrs
   (E) IF FOREIGN BORN, HOW LONG IN THE U.S.A?   YEARS

3. USUAL RESIDENCE OF DECEASED:
   (A) STATE   California
   (B) COUNTY   Los Angeles
   (C) CITY OR TOWN   Los Angeles
   IF OUTSIDE CITY OR TOWN LIMITS, WRITE RURAL
   (D) STREET NO.   6432 Mullholland Highway

20. DATE OF DEATH: MONTH   June   DAY   20th
    YEAR   1948   HOUR   11   MINUTE   15 P.M.

3. (E) IF VETERAN, NAME OF WAR   none
3. (F) SOCIAL SECURITY NO.   none

4. SEX   Male
5. COLOR OR RACE   Caucasian
6. (A) SINGLE, MARRIED, WIDOWED OR DIVORCED   Married

6. (B) NAME OF HUSBAND OR WIFE   Diana Rogers
6. (C) AGE OF HUSBAND OR WIFE IF ALIVE   35 YEARS

7. BIRTHDATE OF DECEASED   March   9   1906
   MONTH   DAY   YEAR
8. AGE   42 YRS   3 MOS   11 DAYS   HRS   MIN
   IF LESS THAN ONE DAY OLD
9. BIRTHPLACE   New York City, New York
10. USUAL OCCUPATION   Manager
11. INDUSTRY OR BUSINESS   Apartment Houses
FATHER
12. NAME   Henry H Rogers
13. BIRTHPLACE   New York
MOTHER
14. MAIDEN NAME   Mary Benjamin
15. BIRTHPLACE   Ogdensburg, New York
16. (A) INFORMANT   Mary Rogers
    (B) ADDRESS   140 West 57th Street New York

17. (A) Temporary Vault   (B) DATE   June 23 1948
    BURIAL, CREMATION, REMOVAL
    (C) PLACE   Forest Lawn Cemetery
18. (A) EMBALMER'S SIGNATURE   Frielzel Hauch   LICENSE NO. 3125
    FOREST LAWN MEMORIAL-PARK ASSOCIATION, INC.
    (B) FUNERAL DIRECTOR
    ADDRESS   GLENDALE, CALIF.
    BY   Robert K. McFresh

    JUN 23 1948
19. (A)   DATE FILED   (B)   REGISTRAR
    Registrar's Signature   DEPUTY REGISTRAR

21. MEDICAL CERTIFICATE
    I HEREBY CERTIFY, THAT I ATTENDED THE DECEASED
    FROM   6-17-48
    TO   6-20-48
    THAT I LAST SAW HIM ALIVE
    ON   6-20-48
    AND THAT DEATH OCCURRED ON THE DATE AND HOUR STATED ABOVE,

    IMMEDIATE CAUSE OF DEATH   Heart failure
    DUE TO   Cirrhosis of the liver (Laennec's)
    DUE TO

    OTHER CONDITIONS
    (INCLUDE PREGNANCY WITHIN THREE MONTHS OF DEATH)

    MAJOR FINDINGS:
    OF OPERATIONS
    DATE OF OPERATION
    OF AUTOPSY   Laennec's Cirrhosis

22. CORONER'S CERTIFICATE
    I HEREBY CERTIFY, THAT I HELD AN
    AUTOPSY, INQUEST OR INVESTIGATION
    ON THE REMAINS OF THE DECEASED AND FIND FROM SUCH ACTION THAT DECEASED CAME TO
    DEATH ON THE DATE AND HOUR

    DURATION   12 hrs
    years

    PHYSICIAN
    UNDERLINE THE CAUSE TO WHICH DEATH SHOULD BE CHARGED STATISTICALLY

23. IF DEATH WAS DUE TO EXTERNAL CAUSES, FILL IN THE FOLLOWING:
    (A) ACCIDENT, SUICIDE, OR HOMICIDE?   (B) DATE OF INJURY
    (C) WHERE DID INJURY OCCUR?   CITY OR TOWN   COUNTY   STATE
    (D) DID INJURY OCCUR IN OR ABOUT HOME, ON FARM, IN INDUSTRIAL PLACE, OR IN PUBLIC PLACE?   SPECIFY TYPE OF PLACE   WHILE AT WORK?
    (E) MEANS OF INJURY

24. CORONER'S OR PHYSICIAN'S SIGNATURE (SPECIFY WHICH)   Hans Schiff, M.D.
    ADDRESS   1680 No. Vine   DATE   6-21-48

STATE OF CALIFORNIA
DEPARTMENT OF PUBLIC HEALTH

CERTIFICATE OF DEATH

FEDERAL SECURITY AGENCY
U.S. PUBLIC HEALTH SERVICE

The last "Henry H. Rogers" of his line,
he was interred beneath his father
and grandfather in Fairhaven.

Freed from her father's influence, Millicent surrounded herself with beautiful clothes, beautiful decor, and handsome men. Her friend Diana Vreeland declared her a style icon—"byzantinely beautiful, independent in taste," with a "sixth sense" for fashion. She became a regular on the list of best-dressed women.

Living in Washington during the war, Millicent had affairs with some of the city's most dashing men, including Undersecretary of the Navy James Forrestal, Ian Fleming, Roald Dahl, and Clark Gable. Millicent followed Clark back to Hollywood, renting Rudolph Valentino's old mansion.

One night, Millicent dropped into Clark's house unannounced—and caught him in bed with a starlet. Heartbroken, Millicent fled to New Mexico, where she discovered the little town of Taos—off the beaten path and home to a small coterie of Bohemians. She fell in love with the landscape and the Pueblo culture.

Millicent went native, dressing in long pleated skirts and heavy turquoise jewelry. She renovated an old adobe house. Alas, her resources—physical and financial—were running out. She began to sell her art and antiques. An old heart condition reasserted itself, forcing her to spend more and more time in bed.

On a frigid Christmas Day, Millicent caught a cold that turned into an infection. She suffered a heart attack and died on New Year's Day of 1953. She was buried in the Taos cemetery.

MILLICENT HUDDLESTON ROGERS
Born Feb. 1. 1902
Died Jan. 1. 1953

The Rogers money passed on
to Henry Huttleston Rogers'
great-grandchildren, who in
turn produced children of their
own and on and on down
through the generations.

And with each new branch in the family tree, the wealth has been divided and diluted. Few of H. H. Rogers' living descendants now face the challenge of having too much money.

But some day, his genes may spawn
another with the Midas touch. Hopefully,
he, or she, will realize that...

$$$ ISN'T EVERYTHING.

The End

Acknowledgements

I could not have completed this project without help from numerous libraries and archives and their staffs. I received crucial assistance from Deb Charpentier, archivist at the beautiful Millicent Library in Fairhaven, Massachusetts. Thanks to Executive Director Gina Wouters at the Planting Fields estate on Long Island, I was able to pore through that institution's voluminous archive of Rogers and Coe family documents. Carmela Quinto at the Millicent Rogers Museum in Taos, New Mexico provided important material on Millicent's time in Taos. In the midst of pandemic lockdowns, Melissa Martin of the Mark Twain Project at the University of California at Berkeley's Bancroft Library managed to secure for me a beautiful image of Twain horsing around with H. H. Rogers in Bermuda. I am particularly grateful, as always, to the New York Public Library for the use of its Wertheim Scholar's Room and the help of staff members Rebecca Federman and Melanie Locay in locating source material. Most of all, I would like to thank my late father, Michael D. Coe, for encouraging me to write about our family's history--and to follow the trail no matter what skeletons I unearthed.

Photo Credits